flourishing & Graceful

flourishing & Graceful

A Praying Guide for Intentional Parents

Esther Ojosemako

Copyright © 2025 Esther Ojosemako

All rights reserved.

No part of this publication may be reproduced, stored in a retrieval system, or transmitted in any form or by any means (electronic, mechanical, photocopying, recording, or otherwise) without the prior written permission of the author, except in the case of brief quotations used in book reviews or articles.

Unless otherwise indicated, all scripture quotations are taken from the New King James Version® (NKJV). Copyright © 1982 by Thomas Nelson. Used by permission. All rights reserved. Scriptures from other translations are clearly noted and credited to their respective sources.

First Edition, 2025
ISBN: 978-1-80605-060-4
Ebook ISBN: 9781806050611
Designed and published by The Esthitude Place
Printed in the United Kingdom

This book is intended for inspirational and educational purposes only. It is not a substitute for professional counselling, therapy, or medical advice. If you or your child requires support in those areas, please consult a qualified professional.
The author has no responsibility for the persistence or accuracy of URLs for external or third-party Internet Websites referred to in this publication and does not guarantee that any content on such Websites is, or will remain, accurate or appropriate.

To every parent who has ever wondered, "Am I doing enough?" This is for you.

And to Samson, my intentional partner in parenting and faithful co-warrior in prayer. Thank you for praying with me and for me.

Contents

ix | Foreword

11 | Introduction

15 | A FAITHFUL FOUNDATION

21 | HOW TO PRAY FOR YOUR CHILDREN

29 | WHEN TO PRAY FOR YOUR CHILDREN

39 | THE POWER OF THE TONGUE

49 | BUILDING YOUR PRAYER ARSENAL

59 | A PRAYER GUIDE

67 | SCRIPTURAL AFFIRMATIONS & PRAYERS FOR YOUR CHILDREN

77 | GENERATIONAL PRAYER LEGACIES

95 | Appendix A: Emergency Prayers for Crisis Situations

102 | Appendix B: Leading Your Child to Christ

105 | Acknowledgement

Foreword

Scripture reminds us that "children are a heritage from the Lord" (Psalm 127:3), entrusted to our care for a season, yet belonging ultimately to God. The responsibility of shaping their hearts and destinies is far too great to be carried in human strength alone. Prayer, therefore, is not optional; it is essential.

As a father, grandfather, and shepherd of many families in the faith, I have learned that one of the greatest gifts we can give our children is the covering of prayer. Over the years, I have regularly reminded parents that prayer is not just a spiritual discipline; it is a destiny-shaping instrument, and it is the means by which we partner with God to shape destinies, protect hearts, and call forth His purposes in the next generation. Yet, in the busyness of life, many parents struggle to pray with focus, consistency, and confidence.

That is why this book is important. Esther, a beloved daughter-in-the-Lord and devoted child of God, has poured her heart, personal journey, and biblical research into these pages. She shares not as one who has "arrived," but as one who is walking the path, learning, growing, and leaning on God daily for wisdom in raising her child. Her authenticity is refreshing, and her insights are both practical and deeply rooted in Scripture.

What you hold in your hands is more than a guide; it is an invitation. An invitation to step into the sacred role God has entrusted to you as a parent, grandparent, or guardian. An invitation to pray with intentionality, to intercede with boldness and to believe God for the impossible in the lives of your children. I believe that as you read, you will be inspired, equipped, and stirred to action.

May this book not only inform your mind but also ignite your spirit to pray without ceasing for the precious lives entrusted to your care, impacting future generations. It is my prayer that generations to come will rise and call you blessed because of the seeds of prayer you sow today.

Pastor (Dr.) Kenny Ademosu.
Regional Overseer, Deeper Life Bible Church, West Midlands, United Kingdom.

Introduction

Do you have any memory of your parents praying for you? Maybe it was your mum laying hands on you at night while you slept, or your dad declaring blessings during family prayer time, or a spontaneous prayer when you called them in distress.

Growing up, it was not uncommon to hear people say things like, "It's my mother's prayers that are sustaining me", or "Thank God for my parents' consistent prayers; if not for them, I don't know where I would be today." These were more than sentiments; they were a recognition of the power and influence of praying parents. One question that constantly echoed in my mind whenever I heard this was, *when we begin to raise children of our own, would they be able to say the same about us?* Will we be praying parents, or will we simply "coast on vibes?"

Parenting is a world of its own. It reshapes your life and recalibrates your priorities. One day, you are focused on just yourself and your spouse, the next, you are staring into the eyes of the cutest little person, entirely dependent on you for food, love, values, and direction. This was my experience, and it brought me to a new reality.

Some hours after my son was born, as we were discharged from the hospital, I had a quiet moment of panic. I thought *"Home? Already? What exactly am I supposed to do? How am I going to care for him?"*

Despite all the books I had read, I realised I needed more than knowledge about feeding, sleep, and schedules. I needed wisdom on how to nurture my son's soul. That moment marked the beginning of an entirely new journey – physical, mental, spiritual, and all-around.

As good parents, we desire to give the best to raise our children well. However, in the rush of daily life, we might overlook something even more important: **caring for their spirit and soul**. The truth is, if we do not intentionally pour into our children's spiritual lives, society, someone, or something else will, and that influence may, most likely, not reflect the values we hold dear or want to see in them.

Introduction

Scripture warns us that the enemy prowls around like a roaring lion, seeking whom he may devour (1 Peter 5:8). Our children are not exempt from his schemes. As parents, we are stewards over our children; therefore, we must ensure that we protect them from every devourer. Through intentional prayers and parenting, we can shield our children by hiding them in God and protecting them from the evil going on in the world.

That is why I wrote this book.

As a new mom caring for my son with my husband, I quickly realised this was not a journey to undertake lightly. I started praying and researching resources to learn how to nurture my child's spiritual growth. This book is a result of prayer, divine inspiration, and research. It aims to help you become intentional in your parenting, especially in shepherding your children's spiritual development.

Because praying for your children must go beyond just saying, "God bless my child." It requires you to speak over their minds, hearts, choices, friendships, identity, and destiny. It requires you to model yieldedness and absolute dependence on God. This book does not just teach you how to pray for your children. It empowers you to **pray aright**—with courage, boldness, wisdom, and intentionality. Through scriptural insight, prayer points, declarations, and spiritual guidance, you will find tools to help you pray with purpose and consistency, whether your children are infants, toddlers, teenagers, or adults.

Let this be your invitation and nudge into the deep. It is time to jointly invest in the lives of those God has entrusted to your care.

Let this be your invitation and nudge into the deep. It is time to jointly invest in the lives of those God has entrusted to your care. Let this be the beginning of a legacy of intentional prayers that shape generations. Amen.

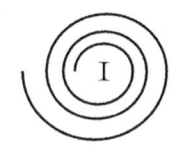

A FAITHFUL FOUNDATION

Behold, children are a heritage from the LORD, the fruit of the womb is a reward.
Psalm 127:3

Parenting is a gift. A blessing. A privilege. A lifetime ministry. And it is likely the toughest job you will ever do. I like to describe it as a sacred, beautiful, messy, and highly rewarding assignment.

Parenting is not just about birthing a child or taking responsibility for one. It holds a deeper resonance. It is embarking on a co-creating journey with God and walking in a lifelong ministry. Fulfilling this ministry cannot be successfully accomplished with our limited understanding; it requires help, prayer, and intentionality.

Intentional parenting is the practice of raising children with purpose, foresight, and a clear set of values. Rather than reacting to every behavioural issue or outsourcing spiritual formation, intentional **Christian** parents plan with the end goal in mind—nurturing faith, character, and compassion that will endure into adulthood. This approach is rooted in the biblical injunction for building a legacy that spans generations.

Train up a child in the way he should go, and when he is old, he will not depart from it. Proverbs 22:6

And these words which I command you today shall be in your heart. You shall teach them diligently to your children, and shall talk of them when you sit in your house, when you walk by the way, when you lie down, and when you rise up. Deuteronomy 6:6,7

As Moses instructed in the passage above, intentional parenting incorporates biblical truth into everyday life, modelling faith, values, and clear, God-honoring boundaries for your children. It asks:
- "What kind of values do I want to see in my child?"
- "How is God calling me to steward my children?"
- "How do I want to model the Christian faith to my children?"

Then aligns every discipline, conversation, and family rhythm toward that goal.

Like Manoah asked the angel of the LORD who prophesied about Samson's birth, *"…Now when your words come true, what is to be the child's manner of life, and what is his mission?"* (Judges 13:12), we must also seek God's face to know His will and plans for our children.

There are many aspects of intentional parenting, but in this book, I will focus on intentional prayers and scriptural parenting. According to 1YoursIntentionally, the 5Ps of intentional parenting are:
- **Pray**: Recognise the need for God's help daily. Turn to God every single day, and ask for His help, His wisdom, and His guidance.
- **Play**: Make time regularly for your children, whether it is shopping together, walking, talking, roller-skating, or playing peekaboo.
- **Praise**: Look for positive traits or characteristics to praise, therefore encouraging more of the behaviour you want to see in them.
- **Protect**: Establish a foundation of trust from their early years and work hard to protect their minds, hearts, and souls from physical, digital, or spiritual predators.
- **Prepare**: Prepare your kids for successful futures, including believing in themselves, having confidence in their abilities, making good choices, knowing what you expect from them, and knowing that God is there to help whenever they need to call on Him.

The primary focus in this book is the first P - **Praying intentionally and effectively as a crucial part of parenting,** a thread that runs through the other Ps mentioned in this intentional parenting framework.

[1]https://yoursintentionally.com/the-5-ps-of-intentional-parenting/

FLOURISHING AND GRACEFUL

Divine Guidance and Support for Parents

The tough news: Parenting ~~can be~~ is a gruelling job.
The best news: You do not have to do it alone; there is HELP.

Yes, you may be tired, angry, fatigued, and stretched more than you think you can bear. Nevertheless, you will also find joy, laughter, growth, and strength more than you ever imagined. God actively equips all who seek to parent according to His design with wisdom, grace, grit, and guidance. Be assured that you are not alone on this parenting journey.

Let this always be your consolation and anchor. Remember this - **parenting is a co-creation journey with God.** So, whenever you feel ill-equipped or unsure in your parenting journey, draw strength from God's Word and from parents who have gone ahead, giving wisdom for the parenting journey.

If any of you lacks wisdom, let him ask of God, who gives to all liberally and without reproach, and it will be given to him. James 1:5

"When I had forgotten God, yet I then found He had not forgotten me. Even then, He did by His Spirit apply the merits of the great atonement to my soul, by telling me that Christ died for me."- Susanna Wesley (mother of John and Charles Wesley)

"If you feel that you do not know how to teach the Word to them, to make

A FAITHFUL FOUNDATION

it interesting or exciting for them, take heart—God will make it come live to them if you are faithful to read it and live it."- Craig T. Owens

God's empowerment, strength, and wisdom for parenting can be experienced through:
1. His indwelling Spirit, who grants patience, wisdom, and compassion far beyond natural ability.
2. His Word, which is "useful for teaching, rebuking, correcting and training in righteousness"
3. The prayerful community of faith, where experienced mentors and co-labourers in Christ offer encouragement and practical insights.

The fact that you are reading this book shows a willingness to grow and do better. I encourage you to read this book with your spouse or parents in your circle and hold yourself accountable on this intentional parenting journey. By parenting with intention, you transition from instinctive firefighting to strategic shepherding of your children's hearts and minds.

> *Prayer is acknowledging and experiencing the presence of God and inviting His presence into our lives and circumstances. It's seeking the presence of God and releasing the power of God which gives us the means to overcome any problem.*
>
> — Stormie Omartian

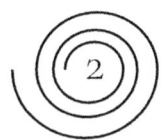

HOW TO PRAY FOR YOUR CHILDREN

Trust in the Lord with all your heart, and lean not on your own understanding; in all your ways acknowledge Him, and He shall direct your paths. Proverbs 3:5,6

Parenting is a beautiful ministry when stewarded in God. Yes, it is stressful and definitely taxing. However, you get the opportunity to collaborate with God in influencing and shaping a human's life. What an honour!

The good news? God is interested in helping you parent right, especially when it comes to guiding your little ones on the path of faith. The spiritual blessings, breakthroughs, and generational grace you give to your children are more than any physical assets you can give to them.

It is important, therefore, to pray for your children, and to become praying parents, you must first understand how to pray, not just in the simple, 'oh God, bless me today' manner, but in a biblically grounded and scripture-based way of praying.

Starting at The Beginning

Praying parents are first praying humans. Simply put, you cannot give what you do not have. As Christians, we pray based on our faith in God and the acceptance of Christ's sacrifice on Calvary.

Therefore, to become a praying parent, the following steps are important:

1. DEVELOP A PERSONAL RELATIONSHIP WITH GOD

    This is the first step to becoming a praying person. Just as you cannot walk up to someone else's parents to ask for an inheritance or access to a trust fund, so also can you not go to God (our heavenly Father) asking for the children's bread if you are not a child of God yourself.

    He replied, "It is not right to take the children's bread and toss it to the dogs." Matthew 15:26 NIV

    God desires a relationship with you. He created you for His glory, and He delights in you and wants to answer all your prayers. However, you must first come to Him and accept His love into your heart, then you can become a child of God.

All that the Father gives Me will come to Me, and the one who comes to Me I will by no means cast out. John 6:37

If you desire to come into a relationship with God today, Jesus is ready to welcome you. All you need to do is:
- confess your sins to Jesus,
- repent of them, and
- accept His finished work of salvation into your life.

You can say this prayer in faith:

Dear God, thank you for your sacrifice of love on the cross of Calvary. I admit that I have sinned (confess your sins to Him), and I need you in my life. I accept your sacrifice of love and surrender my life and ways to you. From today, I confess that You are my Lord and Personal Saviour, in Jesus' name I pray. Amen.

If you prayed this prayer sincerely and in faith, congratulations! **I welcome you to the family of God's beloved people**; indeed, you are welcome to the household of faith.

Next steps:
- Get a physical Bible, or download the YouVersion app

- Start reading the Bible from the Book of Romans, and
- Join a Bible-believing church in your local residence so you can be edified together with the brethren
- You can send me an email, and I'll be happy to share resources with you and pray with you — *estherojosemako@gmail.com*

Welcome again, beloved.

2. DEVELOP A PERSONAL PRAYER LIFESTYLE

You cannot give what you do not have. This means that you cannot pray for your children without having a prayer life yourself. Unfortunately, this is one aspect of life you cannot delegate to others, not your church, and definitely not the school.

You must first develop a prayer life before you can become intentional and consistent in praying for your children. To achieve this, you need to:
- Pray regularly
- Read scriptures on prayers
- Have dedicated prayer times
- Leverage the power of corporate prayers (with your partner or through corporate prayer programs)
- Keep a prayer journal
- Pray everywhere at all times

Children are like sponges; they watch and absorb things around them quickly. **You cannot teach them to be prayerful when they have not seen you model a**

consistent prayer life.
3. SIMPLY START
Start from conception, start when they are babies, start before they are born. Just start. Do not wait until your children are old before you start praying for them.

Here is how you can start:
- Before conception:
  - Sending prayers and affirmation into their future
  - Journaling specific instructions from God about them
  - Growing deeper in God and becoming better at praying
- During pregnancy:
  - Same as above, and
  - By laying your hands on your (partner's) pregnant tummy and declaring safety and ease over the foetus
- As they grow:
  - By daily praying over them as they prepare for school
  - By praying over needs or issues in the house together
  - By having them around during your personal prayer time

Do not overthink it, just start, and from there, you can build consistency.

4. **PRAY THE WORD**
   One powerful way to pray for your children is by leveraging the Word of God, i.e., the Scriptures.

For the word of God is living and powerful, and sharper than any two-edged sword, piercing even to the division of soul and spirit, and of joints and marrow, and is a discerner of the thoughts and intents of the heart.
Hebrews 4:12

And they overcame him by the blood of the Lamb and by the word of their testimony, and they did not love their lives to the death.
Revelations 12:11

Whether it is the Book of Psalms, the Beatitude, or Paul's prayer, you can pick any of these Scriptures as a reference to pray over your ward.

A practical example:
Bible Passage
For this reason we also, since the day we heard it, do not cease to pray for you, and to ask that you may be filled with the knowledge of His will in all wisdom and spiritual understanding; that you may walk worthy of the Lord, fully pleasing Him, being fruitful in every good work and increasing in the knowledge of God;
Colossians 1:9-10

Prayer for your child from this Bible Passage
Father, give [your child's name] a complete knowledge

of Your will in all spiritual wisdom and understanding. Then [child's name] will live and always honour and please You, and [his/her] life will produce every kind of good fruit. All their days, [child's name] will grow as they learn to know God better and better.

What this means
You personalise the scriptures as the basis of your prayer for your children, replacing the pronouns with your children's name, and activating the scripture on their behalf. No more leaving their life to chance; it is time to pray the Word over them literally.

Chapter 7 is dedicated to this concept, with practical examples and templates for praying for your children

5. KEEP AT IT
There may be days or seasons when you do not feel like praying or when it seems like there is no answer in sight. Even then, keep praying. Remember the Syrophenician woman? She kept petitioning Jesus for her child until she got a favourable response from Him.

For a woman whose young daughter had an unclean spirit heard about Him, and she came and fell at His feet. The woman was a Greek, a Syro-Phoenician by birth, and she kept asking Him to cast the demon out of her daughter. But Jesus said to her, "Let the children be filled first, for it is not good to take the children's bread and throw it to the little dogs."
And she answered and said to Him, "Yes, Lord, yet even the little dogs under the table eat from the children's crumbs."

Then He said to her, "For this saying go your way; the demon has gone out of your daughter." Mark 7:25-29

6. **PRAY WITH YOUR CHILDREN**
   Children learn the fastest through observation and hands-on experience. Whether they are toddlers or teenagers, it is important to start involving your children in prayers. Ask your little one to say a prayer before meals, or have your teenager lead the family devotion prayers. Whatever way this applies to you, involve your children in prayers early on.

   This way, you not only get to pray with your children, but you also empower them to become praying children and later, praying parents.

7. **KEEP A PRAYER JOURNAL**
   Prayer journals are not just keepsakes; they serve as memorials and living testimonies of your faith by tracking answered prayers over the years. You can strengthen your children's faith by maintaining a family prayer journal in which you record prayer requests, express gratitude and thanksgiving, and note answered prayers together.
   You can get either a blank journal from a store close to you or a dedicated prayer journal. If you prefer a dedicated prayer journal, I have one that you can get on Amazon[2].

---

[2] Search for Guided Prayer Journal by Esther Ojosemako on Amazon

WHEN TO PRAY FOR YOUR CHILDREN

I want everyone everywhere to lift innocent hands toward heaven and pray, without being angry or arguing with each other.
1 Timothy 2:8 CEV

Short Answer: Every day. Even before they are born.
Detailed Answer: While today's worldview suggests you cannot predict how your child will turn out, your story can be different as a Christian. By the grace of God, through the guidance of the Holy Spirit, and with encouragement and accountability, you can influence your children's development. Yes, there may be exceptions, but with prayers, these exceptions can be turned around for good.

Prayer is both a covering and a weapon. It is an essential

tool that every intentional parent should have in his/her parenting arsenal.

If you are reading this as a parent genuinely concerned about raising your child purposefully in this age and time, you are in good company. If you are reading this as a parent-to-be, hoping to one day have little ones of your own, this is the right book for you.

Growing up, my mum often said, "pray into your future before you arrive there." She would pray for us and encourage us to pray about our marriage and future children from a young age. Even though I did not fully understand it then, I appreciate it now, and I still use that strategy in every area of my life.

Before you start having children, and even if you are still single, it is important to pray not only for your future partner but also for your unborn children. This serves as an investment in the bank of your future. Also, couples trying to conceive or waiting to have their babies can start praying for them before they arrive.

Once after a sacrificial meal at Shiloh, Hannah got up and went to pray. Eli the priest was sitting at his customary place beside the entrance of the Tabernacle. Hannah was in deep anguish, crying bitterly as she prayed to the Lord. And she made this vow: "O Lord of Heaven's Armies, if you will look upon my sorrow and answer my prayer and give me a son, then I will give him back to you. He will be yours for his entire lifetime, and as a sign that he has been dedicated to the Lord, his hair will never be cut. 1 Samuel 1:9-11 NLT

Delay is never denial. If God is taking time to prepare you for parenting, rejoice in the waiting room. Like Hannah, Abraham and Sarah, Elizabeth and John, God is preparing greatness to be birthed through your loins.

On Praying Frequency

Now Jesus was telling the disciples a parable to make the point that at all times they ought to pray and not give up and lose heart. Luke 18:1 AMP

Pray without ceasing. I Thessalonians 5:17

And pray in the Spirit on all occasions with all kinds of prayers and requests. With this in mind, be alert and always keep on praying for all the Lord's people. Ephesians 6:18 NLT

These Scriptures serve as the foundational basis of how often Christians should pray. It is even more important to embrace this as parents who do not want to leave the destiny of their children to chance.

You should pray at all times. And everywhere.

Praying for your children should be a joint effort. When a couple agrees in prayer, it multiplies the impact. The praying responsibility should not be left to a particular gender or parent.

FLOURISHING AND GRACEFUL

For where two or three are gathered together in My name, I am there in the midst of them. Matthew 18:20

Confess your trespasses to one another, and pray for one another, that you may be healed. The effective, fervent prayer of a righteous man avails much. James 5:16

When a couple jointly agree over their children, the results are undeniable.

So, When Should You Pray for Your Children?

Pray for them:
- As expecting parents, waiting on God for children.
- As fetuses, growing in the womb.
- As infants who do not understand what you are saying.
- At home, before heading to school.
- At home, before going to sleep.
- When they are healthy, living their life.
- When they are ill or poorly.
- When they have tests or exams.
- When they are grown and living on their own.
- When they become parents and have their children.
- Every time. Everywhere. Everyday.

WHEN TO PRAY FOR YOUR CHILDREN

As intentional parents, you should never stop praying for your children. Praying for your children is a lifelong ministry. To date, my parents still pray for me and my siblings, and now that I am a parent myself, I cherish more dearly their prayers for me and my family.

Creating A System for Intentional And Effective Prayers

As someone big on goal setting and systems, I find that having a prayer system helps with consistency and aids intentionality in prayer.

First, what is a system? A system is a set of principles or procedures according to which something is done. In a busy world with many things fighting for your attention, having a repeatable procedure is setting yourself up for success as a praying parent.

Here are practical steps on how you can systematically make praying for your children a lifestyle.

1. SCHEDULE PRAYER TIMES EVERY MORNING.
   No matter how busy in a hurry you are, always ensure to say a prayer over your children every morning. When they are still living with you, try as much as possible to include them in the prayers, even if they do not understand it yet. The length or duration is not as important as the heart and content of prayer, so say a

prayer over them every day before heading out.

2. ATTACH PRAYERS TO AN ACTIVITY YOU ALWAYS DO.
What is an activity you do regularly? Driving? Cooking? Sending emails? Whatever it is for you, you can attach prayers/praying for your children to this task. This way, you are ensuring you pray for them every day while getting your daily tasks done.

Another email sent. A quick whispered prayer. *"Thank You God for my son, may he thrive in his academics and have great interpersonal skills. Amen."*

It could be that every time you start your car, change their diaper, pack their school lunch, or before you open your laptop for the day, you say a prayer for them. For instance, I committed to praying for children (not just mine) every time I document in my prayer journal.

Attaching prayer to a daily task makes it easier to do and track, knowing that it is not how long, but how well.

3. PRAY FOR/WITH THEM EVERY NIGHT.
Whether they are with you or have left home, a whisper of prayer for safety and protection each night goes a long way. Read a scripture with them and pray over them every night; with this, you pass on a spiritual legacy and tradition that can be sown for future generations.

WHEN TO PRAY FOR YOUR CHILDREN

Instead of reading generic stories to them at night, read Bible stories and even the Bible to them. They may not fully understand it yet, but it is sowing a seed, and keeping you on my toes.

4. HAVE DEDICATED PRAYER TIMES FOR THEM AND WITH THEM

Create a regular schedule to pray for your children, either alone, with your partner, children, or an accountability group. This can be weekly or monthly. I suggest choosing consistency in the long term and leveraging technology to automate the process.

Here is a practice that works for me – **automation.** I use a digital calendar or alarm to set up a recurring meeting. This helps me stay accountable. I also have a prayer group with some friends, and we meet just once a month to pray for our families.

One of my pastors mentioned that he always prays at midnight, and when his daughter asked him about it, he invited her to join him whenever she is awake. Now, she joins him whenever she is awake. What better example of simply and systematically living out our faith and influencing our children to do the same?

5. DISCERNING AND PRAYING IN TIMES OF TROUBLE

Have you ever experienced a situation where you were going through a tough time, facing a temptation, or needed to make a major decision, and then your parent called you "out of the blue" to pray for you or tell you about a dream they had about you? That is discernment.

As co-creators with God, parents are sometimes able to discern when something is about to happen to their children, good or bad. It could be through dreams, visions, or a nudge in the spirit. When this happens, do not give in to fear. I have learned from my parents that this is a time to pray, either to receive/activate a blessing or refute/rescind an evil occurrence.

When praying for your children, do not be afraid to seek help in prayers from an accountability circle, your partner, a trusted mentor or pastor, or your parents. These little drops of water, or better put, prayers, are like investing; you may not see the returns now, but they will yield and usually in multiple folds.

Is anyone among you suffering? Let him pray. Is anyone cheerful? Let him sing psalms.
Is anyone among you sick? Let him call for the elders of the church, and let them pray over him, anointing him with oil in the name of the Lord.
And the prayer of faith will save the sick, and the Lord will raise him up. And if he has committed sins, he will be forgiven.
Confess your trespasses to one another, and pray for one another, that you may be healed. The effective, fervent prayer of a righteous man avails much. James 5:13-16

WHEN TO PRAY FOR YOUR CHILDREN

Benefits Of Intentional Prayers for Your Children

Prayer is the cornerstone of intentional parenting because it invites God's supernatural work into every aspect of a child's life.

Praying specifically and regularly for children:
- Builds a strong spiritual foundation, helping them understand their identity in Christ and fostering resilience in adversity.
- Develops coping skills by reducing anxiety and instilling peace beyond human understanding.
- Encourages purpose and direction, guiding them to discover and steward their unique gifts for God's glory.
- Strengthens parent-child bonds, as shared prayer times become moments of vulnerability, listening, and mutual trust.

By weaving prayer into daily routines like mealtimes, bedtime, or car rides, you demonstrate dependence on God and model lifelong spiritual habits. This intentional intercession not only petitions God for your children's needs but also transforms your heart.

Pray when you feel like it, and when you don't.

"
Our purpose as parents is clearly defined here: we are to make disciples. That includes our children. I'd argue that, for parents, our children are our priority in making disciples. The great commission begins in the home.

Chris Swain

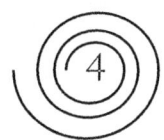

THE POWER OF THE TONGUE

The tongue has the power of life and death, and those who love it will eat its fruit. Proverbs 18:21 NIV

The tongue, though tiny, is a powerful body asset. Just as it has multiple functions as an organ, it can also have various effects in its usage.

For we all stumble in many things. If anyone does not stumble in word, he is a perfect man, able also to bridle the whole body. James 3:2

The tongue also is a fire, a world of evil among the parts of the body. It corrupts the whole body, sets the whole course of one's life on fire, and is itself set on fire by hell. James 3:6 NIV

FLOURISHING AND GRACEFUL

You must know that there is power in the words you speak. With the Word, God created the heavens and the earth, and with your words, you can mould generations or destroy them. Therefore, it is important to watch the words you speak, especially as a parent.

First, I need to emphasise that you cannot pray for your children and hope they will become great while also cursing them or speaking unedifying words over them, whether consciously or unconsciously. I agree that even for the most loving parents, it requires grace, determination, and intentionality not to speak harmful words over their children, especially when they are doing things they should not. Nevertheless, it is possible; this is why you must be careful, discerning, and intentional.

The devil takes advantage of moments when you are angry, frustrated, overwhelmed or displeased, to trigger you to speak in anger. Before you know it, you may start to see the traits of these words in your child's life. May this not be your case, in Jesus' name. Amen.

"Oh, but I was only joking!"

Here is what the Bible has to say:
But I tell you that men will give an account on the day of judgment for every careless word they have spoken. For by your words you will be acquitted, and by your words you will be condemned. Matthew 12:36,37

Let no foul or polluting language, nor evil word nor unwholesome or worthless talk [ever] come out of your mouth, but only such [speech] as is good and beneficial to the spiritual progress of others, as is fitting to the need and the occasion, that it may be a blessing and give grace (God's favor) to those who hear it. Ephesians 4:29 AMPC

"Don't mind this one; she is a foolish child."
"My child is naturally stubborn; he cannot change."

Statements like these, typically spoken without much thought and intended to do no harm, when said repeatedly, can form the basis of unwanted traits in a child. They give the devil and his minions a legal ground for implanting such behaviours in that child. This is why you must be intentional in the way you or anyone else speak to or about your child. Even when playing, you must be conscious and intentional about your choice of words.

He who has knowledge restrains and is careful with his words, And a man of understanding and wisdom has a cool spirit (self-control, an even temper). Proverbs 17:27 AMP

Learning from God's Example

We were all once sinners separated from God because of our iniquities, yet God loved us and spoke words that would draw us to Him. He sends His Word to us through different means, reminding us repeatedly about who He created us to be and the relationship He wants to have with us.

He sent His word and healed them, And delivered them from their destructions. Psalms 107:20
Once you were alienated from God and were enemies in your minds

because of your evil behaviour. But now he has reconciled you by Christ's physical body through death to present you holy in his sight, without blemish and free from accusation Colossians 1:21-22 NIV

From God, we learn the importance of repeated affirmations. Despite our sinful nature, He still extends His love to us, affirming His love for us repeatedly throughout His Word. The question is: Are you following God's example?

It starts with you:
- How do you speak to yourself?
- How do you speak when addressing other people?
- Are you quick to speak down on yourself?
- Are you quick to use abusive words?
- Are you quick to name-call, shame, and blame others?
- Are you quick to use foul words?

These foundational issues have to be fixed first. You need to:
- Repent from every foul speaking
- Receive grace to speak only edifying words
- Practice and practice and practice
- Be accountable to your partner, pastor, mentor, or coach

If you have been speaking mindlessly to your children, first, you need to stop it, and then you can reverse any evil words or curses previously uttered. As a parent, you have the authority, in God, to cancel negative utterances and speak new realities over your child. It will require prayer, patience, and divine wisdom, but it can happen, and it will happen by God's grace.

If you have a recalcitrant child, like the prodigal child in the Bible, your child will come to himself/herself and will turn a new leaf. And when it seems like the child is not changing or showing the desired positive attitude, do not stop praying for them.

In addition, here are some things you can do:
- Pray for them in your secret place
- Pray out loud for them when they can hear
- Speak words of love and affirmation over them even when they are wrong. Of course, there should still be discipline, but it should be done within the lens of love and to draw the child back in.
- Remove foul or unedifying words from your vocabulary at all times
- Constantly remind them that you love them
- Speak positively to and over them, addressing them the way you want them to turn out
- Ask for help. Pray to God, and, when needed, engage a counsellor, pastor, or mentor to guide you

But as for you, brethren, do not grow weary in doing good.
II Thessalonians 3:13

Finally, brethren, whatever things are true, whatever things are noble, whatever things are just, whatever things are pure, whatever things are lovely, whatever things are of good report, if there is any virtue and if there is anything praiseworthy—meditate on these things. Philippians 4:8
Let Philippians 4:8 serve as a guide when speaking to yourself,

your children, or anyone. If you notice you speak uncontrollably when angry, it is best to keep quiet when angry or triggered than speak without thinking. Hold your peace and address the situation when you are calm.

Be mindful of what you say at all times. Do not jokingly speak evil over your child, even by illustration or songs. I take this very seriously. From when I was a child, I would cry if anyone cursed or cussed at me, and as I got older, I learned to repudiate such words immediately.

Intentionality in The Little Things

On one of the days, when my baby was still an infant, I was trying to soothe him as he cried, so I started singing an old children's song:

I have a little cough, sir
In my little chest, sir
Every time I cough, sir
It gives a little hmmph, sir

At this time, my baby was fine; he did not have a cough and was not ill. I sang this song mindlessly, and I remember laughing with my husband about the song because it was such an old song that came to mind. A few days later, my baby came down with a severe cough and cold that stayed for weeks. It took prayers and many sleepless nights before he got better.

While there may be nothing wrong with this nursery rhyme in itself, and you may choose to see this as a coincidence, it reinforced to me the power of our words and the impact they can have.

> *"What if it was a coincidence?"*
> *"But, what if it wasn't?"*
> *"What if the mindless words gave cough an avoidable foothold?"*

Why can't we sing edifying lullabies to our children?

Another simple example is one time when I was talking to a friend on the phone, and I could hear her child fussing in the background. Asking her what the issue was, she told me that her child had been refusing to eat. I advised her to try praying instead of worrying. Still on the call, a few moments later, she responded, it worked. Yes, it worked because she channelled her parental influence the right way.

These examples, though seemingly simple and basic, are used intentionally to serve as a foundation you can build on with faith and prayers. I have had many more scenarios where I had to be mindful of the words I use, just as you may have too, but it starts from the simple things, which are sometimes the hardest to do.

> *Let your speech always be gracious, seasoned with salt, so that you may know how you should answer each person. Colossians 4:6 CSB*

Speaking over Every Part of Your Child's Body

Earlier, I reiterated the need to speak positively to your children. As good as this can sound, it can sometimes be overwhelming.

"What should I say?"
"I've said everything that comes to mind. What else is there to pray?"
"I'm not sure where to start."

Meanwhile, the moment we get tired in the waiting, God's Spirit is right alongside helping us along. If we don't know how or what to pray, it doesn't matter. He does our praying in and for us, making prayer out of our wordless sighs, our aching groans. He knows us far better than we know ourselves, knows our pregnant condition, and keeps us present before God. That's why we can be so sure that every detail in our lives of love for God is worked into something good. Romans 8:26-28 MSG

While there is no one specific way to pray over our children, we have the gift of the Holy Spirit to guide us on what and how to pray over them.

One method the Holy Spirit taught me is what I call **The Parts of the Body Prayers**. This method, as the name implies, involves praying, speaking, and affirming God's Word over every part of your child.

How it works:

Mention every part of your child's body and pray or affirm

God's word over them. From their head to their toes, as much as you can, you declare the realities you want to see, and you can go as granular as you want. I will use the head as an example.

Speaking over your child's head:

With this method, you focus on every part of the child's head and pray over it.

Head - [Child's Name], your head is covered by God. No evil is allowed to befall you. You are anointed by God, and your head will never lack oil in Jesus' name.

Brain - Your brain functions at its most optimal state. You will not be dysfunctional. We receive wisdom and grace to feed you with the best food to develop your brain.

Eyes - You see properly, physically and spiritually. Your vision is clear. You discern people and situations with precision. You will never lose your eyesight. Your sight will not grow dim. You will not watch evil things - no porn, no dirty games, videos or social media pages in Jesus' name. Amen

Ears - With your ears, you hear the voice of the Lord, and you follow God's leading. No ear infections are allowed. You heed godly instructions and obey in Jesus' name. Amen

Nose - Your nose works perfectly. The breath of God is in you. Your nose will not be pierced with a snare in Jesus' name. Amen

Mouth - Your teeth, tongue, lips, and mouth are God's. You utter words in righteousness. You speak with kindness, authority, and wisdom. Your voice is heard in the nations. Your voice will not be used to serve the devil. You will not speak lies in Jesus' name. Amen

You can get as granular as you want. Pray for their minds, that they discern between good and evil; that they choose what is right, and meditate on that which is pure. Extend the prayers to their hands, back, spine, stomach, legs, reproductive organs, and feet. There is so much to pray over them when you pray this way.

I have found this method of praying for my child helpful.

Feel free to adapt this prayer method as you find suitable and always ask the Holy Spirit to help as you pray. He is ever willing to help.

BUILDING YOUR PRAYER ARSENAL

For the weapons of our warfare are not carnal but mighty in God for pulling down strongholds,. 2 Corinthians 10:4

Praying for your children is similar to going to war for them. Tackling any foundational or future issues on your knees, even before they manifest. Clearing the path for them, settling their future in God, as Abraham did.

Fathers, do not provoke your children to anger [do not exasperate them to the point of resentment with demands that are trivial or unreasonable or humiliating or abusive; nor by showing favouritism or indifference to any of them], but bring them up [tenderly, with lovingkindness] in the discipline and instruction of the Lord. Ephesians 6:4 AMP

This scripture typifies how to bring up children in the right way, leveraging the tools/weapons of love, discipline, and the Word. You are to ensure to teach them the Word of God.

Important Weapons in Every Diligent Parent's Prayer Arsenal

The weapons we fight with are not the weapons of the world. On the contrary, they have divine power to demolish strongholds. We demolish arguments and every pretension that sets itself up against the knowledge of God, and we take captive every thought to make it obedient to Christ. And we will be ready to punish every act of disobedience, once your obedience is complete. 2 Corinthians 10: 4-6 NIV

As this passage explains, the war we are fighting as believers and as parents is not physical, and so our weapons cannot be physical weapons like guns or swords; instead, we are to wield spiritual weapons like faith, prayers, and praise.

Children today are faced with so many issues and challenges, from learning struggles, addiction, medical and mental health issues, to spiritual battles and developmental issues. There is so much that the school, hospitals or society can do for them; we must ensure that we cover our children with prayers, and we can only do this effectively when we are equipped with the right tools/weapons.

Ephesians 6:13-18 describes some of the weapons needed in our prayer arsenal.

[13] Wherefore take unto you the whole armour of God, that ye may be

able to withstand in the evil day, and having done all, to stand.
[14] Stand therefore, having your loins girt about with truth, and having on the breastplate of righteousness;
[15] and your feet shod with the preparation of the gospel of peace;
[16] above all, taking the shield of faith, wherewith ye shall be able to quench all the fiery darts of the wicked.
[17] And take the helmet of salvation, and the sword of the Spirit, which is the word of God:
[18] praying always with all prayer and supplication in the Spirit, and watching thereunto with all perseverance and supplication for all saints;

The armour of God, as described in this passage, contains both defensive and offensive units.

With the **defensive units** - such as the helmet, breastplate, and shield of faith - we protect our family, our home, and ourselves.

With the **offensive units** - such as the sword of the Spirit and prayer - we fight the enemy, ensuring that our loved ones and we are protected at all times.

Unpacking the weapons in our armour:
1. BELT OF TRUTH

    A belt holds our clothes in place, preventing our nakedness from being exposed. As parents, we must uphold truth and integrity in all we do, at home, in our places of work, and everywhere we find ourselves. Not only are we pleasing God this way, but we are also laying the right foundation for our children, ensuring that they are upheld by the right values.

2. BREASTPLATE OF RIGHTEOUSNESS
   Worn on the chest, the breastplate serves as a protection from every attack against our family or us. It serves as a moral guide, too, because it is a cover for our hearts, shielding us from evil thoughts, ideas, or initiatives. Choose righteousness as your way of life.

3. SHOES OF EVANGELISM/PEACE
   As parents, we must be peacemakers and our children's first priests and pastors. We cannot leave the salvation of our children to chance or even the church. You must be the first evangelist to your children, mirroring Christ in the way you live and in all you do.
   Your home should be a haven for your children, where Jesus is the centre and the peace and love of God are exemplified.

4. SHIELD OF FAITH
   Faith is a shield that protects our minds and our children from every evil attack, whether it is mental, physical, or spiritual.

Why worry when you can pray?
Why allow doubt or fear when you can have faith in God?

Stop allowing fear, worry, or doubt to rule the thoughts you have over your children; instead, have faith in God, who gave them to you, that He will keep them and watch over them.

5. HELMET OF SALVATION
Salvation is the reason we have God's covering over us and our family. Through salvation, we become God's adopted children, and the evil one cannot exert control over us. If you are reading this and have not surrendered your all to Jesus, I encourage you to yield your life to God. That is the only way to live and win as an individual and as a family.

6. SWORD OF THE SPIRIT
This is the Word of God, and in the following chapters, I dive deeper into how we can use the Word as a weapon.

7. PRAYING AND WATCHING
We cannot but pray and watch over our little ones (whether they are still at home with us or are now living on their own). We must lift them in prayers daily, covering them in God, and this is the central focus of this book.

Other weapons highlighted to us through the Scriptures include:

8. THE BLOOD OF JESUS
The Blood of Jesus is efficacious in washing away our sins and protecting us from all evil. Praying for your children to be saved or be protected from every evil? Wield the Blood of Jesus as a weapon.

[11] But Christ came as High Priest of the good things to come,

with the greater and more perfect tabernacle not made with hands, that is, not of this creation.

[12] Not with the blood of goats and calves, but with His own blood He entered the Most Holy Place once for all, having obtained eternal redemption.

[13] For if the blood of bulls and goats and the ashes of a heifer, sprinkling the unclean, sanctifies for the purifying of the flesh,

[14] how much more shall the blood of Christ, who through the eternal Spirit offered Himself without spot to God, cleanse your conscience from dead works to serve the living God?
Hebrews 9:11-14

9. THE NAME OF JESUS

Teach your children to call on the name of Jesus whenever they need help, whether you are there or not. Teach them about the power in the name of Jesus.

[9] Therefore God also has highly exalted Him and given Him the name which is above every name,
[10] that at the name of Jesus every knee should bow, of those in heaven, and of those on earth, and of those under the earth,
[11] and that every tongue should confess that Jesus Christ is Lord, to the glory of God the Father.
Philippians 2:9-11

10. LOVE

Yes, love is a weapon too. Breaking down the walls of barriers between parents and children. The perfect example of how love breaks down our walls is God. God is love, and because of His love for us, He sent

His son to die for our sins, breaking down the wall separating us and granting us access to eternal life.
Love, wisdom, and discipline are great weapons needed to raise goodly and godly children.

[4] Love suffers long and is kind; love does not envy; love does not parade itself, is not puffed up;
[5] does not behave rudely, does not seek its own, is not provoked, thinks no evil;
[6] does not rejoice in iniquity, but rejoices in the truth;
[7] bears all things, believes all things, hopes all things, endures all things.
[8] Love never fails. But whether there are prophecies, they will fail; whether there are tongues, they will cease; whether there is knowledge, it will vanish away.
I Corinthians 13:4-8

11. PRAISE

Splashed across the Bible, from the Old to the New Testament, we see how, through praise and thanksgiving, the enemies were discomfited, chains were broken, and food multiplied.
If you are getting weary in prayer and are not sure how to pray again for your children, switch to praise and thanksgiving, and watch God fight your battles for you.

[21] And when he had consulted with the people, he appointed those who should sing to the Lord, and who should praise the beauty of holiness, as they went out before the army and were saying: "Praise the Lord, For His mercy endures forever."
[22] Now when they began to sing and to praise, the Lord set

ambushes against the people of Ammon, Moab, and Mount Seir, who had come against Judah; and they were defeated.
II Chronicles 20:21-22

12. ANOINTING OIL

I saved this for last because this may be classified as a 'physical weapon of protection'. From the Old to the New Testament, the anointing oil was used to dedicate a place or person, to pray for the sick, and to consecrate a people.

Before embarking on a journey, at the commencement of a new school term, when you move into a new house, or if your children are poorly, you can anoint them with oil, as a mark of the blood of Jesus, praying for protection, preservation, healing, or dedication to God.

Is anyone among you sick? Let him call for the elders of the church, and let them pray over him, anointing him with oil in the name of the Lord. James 5:14

Always be clothed in white, and always anoint your head with oil. Ecclesiastes 9:8 NIV

And they cast out many demons, and anointed with oil many who were sick, and healed them. Mark 6:13

BUILDING YOUR PRAYER ARSENAL

Practical Steps for Today's Parents: Building A Prayer Legacy

As your prayer arsenal is built, developed, and deployed, the goal should be to leave a legacy that outlasts you, just as we learn from Abraham, Isaac, and Israel (Jacob).

- Cultivate Your Own Relationship with God: Your children's spiritual inheritance begins with your personal walk with God. Before you pray for your children, pray for yourself, that you would know God deeply, love Him wholly, and walk with Him faithfully.

- Pray Specifically and Persistently for Each Child: Get to know your children, their unique personalities, struggles, gifts, and purposes, and pray accordingly. Create a prayer list for each child that includes:
    - Their relationship with God (salvation, devotion, spiritual growth)
    - Their character development (integrity, wisdom, courage, compassion)
    - Their unique gifts and calling
    - Their future spouse and children
    - Protection from evil and temptation

- Verbalise Your Faith and God's Promises: Do not assume your children will absorb your faith by osmosis. Pray with your children, not just for them. Let them hear you intercede for them, thank God for them, and declare

God's promises over them.

- Connect Present Faithfulness to Future Generations: Help your children understand that their walk with God will impact their children and grandchildren. When praying for your children, include prayers for your future grandchildren and great-grandchildren. Teach your children to think generationally about their faith and choices.

- Trust God's Covenant Faithfulness: Both Abraham and David died before seeing the full fulfilment of God's promises. Release your children to God, trusting that He loves them more than you do and that His plans for them are good. Pray with faith, not fear.

- Partner with Grandparents: Lois's influence on Timothy was profound. If your children's grandparents walk with God, invite their involvement in your children's spiritual formation. If you are a grandparent, recognise that your role is not secondary; you have a unique influence and opportunity.

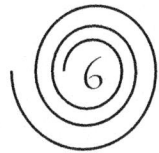

A PRAYER GUIDE

All your children shall be taught by the LORD, and great shall be the peace of your children.
Isaiah 54:13

This chapter is dedicated especially to new parents. I started writing it shortly after having my baby and looking for a guide on how to pray for my child beyond everyday "God bless and keep you". If you are a parent of older children, you can also adapt the prayers to suit your current realities.

Below are specially curated prayer points across different areas of parenting to guide you as you pray. It is by no means an exhaustive list; rather, see it as a guide on days when you need pointers on praying for your children.

You can also print them out to pray daily. I suggest you read out the prayers as you speak over your children.

The blank spaces are for you to fill in more prayers straight from your heart, in your own words. Use this as regularly as you need it and come back to it as often as you want.

THANKSGIVING

- Dear God, I thank you for the honour and opportunity to be a parent.
- I thank you for my children, for they are like mighty arrows ready to be used for your glory in our family and in their generation.
- Thank you, dear God, for the opportunity to co-parent with You.

Add yours

A PRAYER GUIDE

FOR PARENTING GOD'S WAY

- I receive grace and wisdom, as a faithful steward, to parent rightly in God.
- I receive all the resources I need to take care of my children.
- I submit to God on this parenting journey, and I model godly living to my children.
- I will live long enough to take care of my children.

FOR WISDOM & GUIDANCE

- Dear God, grant [child's name] heavenly wisdom and spiritual understanding. Let Your Word be a lamp to their feet and a light to their path; may they lean not on their own understanding but acknowledge You in all their ways, and You will direct their steps

FOR SALVATION, SPIRITUAL GROWTH, AND LIFE'S FULFILMENT

- Dear God, you have ordained my children's days and prepared a purpose for them before they were born. Grant them revelation to know their calling and the boldness to step into all You have destined.
- My children will know and serve the Lord from a young age in Jesus' name. They will be godly, and not just good, in Jesus' name.
- The Spirit of God dwells in you, and like Timothy, you will know the way of the Lord from your childhood.
- [Child's name], I dedicate you to God the Father, the Son, and the Holy Spirit.
- Like Jeremiah, you, [child's name], are called of God from the womb, and you will fulfil your divine destiny.
- [Child's name], I speak God's mercy and grace over you all through your life's journey.
- Your good works will point others to Christ, and no one will be able to diminish the light that you are.
- God is gracious and merciful to my children always.
- You, [child's name], will delight in prayer, worship, and meditating on Scripture. May you grow in grace and in the knowledge of our Lord and Saviour, equipped to run the race marked out for you.
- You will not follow the multitude to do evil. When sinners entice you, you will not consent to them. Amen.

A PRAYER GUIDE

FOR PROTECTION, PRESERVATION, AND PROVISION

- [Child' name], you are a unique child created in the image of God to show forth His glory, and so, no weapon formed against you shall prosper, and no evil shall befall you all your days.
- You will grow and achieve all your developmental milestones at the right time.
- You are blessed of God and highly favoured.
- You shall live and not die to declare the works of the Lord in the land of the living.
- You shall be the head and not the tail, you shall be above and not beneath.
- The Lord perfects all that concerns you, as you grow and develop; I declare nothing broken, nothing missing in you in Jesus' name.
- You are the light of the World, and so I speak over you that you will shine brightly in your generation.
- Because all the children God has given me are for signs and wonders, you, my child, and all your siblings will be a sign and wonder to your world. The world will marvel at the greatness that you are and embody.
- Your mind is protected from evil at all times.
- Your every need is richly supplied according to God's glorious riches.
- May you find favour with God and with all who encounter you, and may God's hand go with you in every endeavour. Amen.

FOR EDUCATION & APTITUDE

- Dear God, grant [child's name] diligence and discernment in study. May the eyes of the Lord be upon them for good, equipping them with skill, creativity, and a quick mind for every task.

FOR RELATIONSHIPS & FRIENDSHIPS

- I pray that [child's name] chooses friends wisely, they will walk with the wise and become wise, and find companions who sharpen their faith. Fill their heart to love others as Christ loves them

A PRAYER GUIDE

FOR CHARACTER & INTEGRITY

- You, [child's name], will walk in integrity. Your 'yes' will be yes, and your 'no' will be no, that you may stand blameless before God and man.

FOR EMOTIONAL & MENTAL WELL-BEING

- Dear God, guard the mind and heart of my children. May Your peace, which surpasses all understanding, keep them in Christ Jesus, and may they cast every anxiety on You, for You care deeply for them.

- You, [child's name], will be filled with the joy of the Lord, which is your strength. In trials, you will stand firm, knowing that suffering produces perseverance, character, and hope.

FOR FUTURE SPOUSE & FAMILY LIFE

- Lord, prepare [child's name] a partner after Your own heart. Guard their purity until marriage and bless them to build a home founded on Your Word, a home of love, faith, and mutual honour

Add more prayers

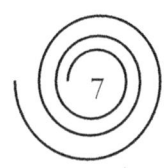

SCRIPTURAL AFFIRMATIONS & PRAYERS FOR YOUR CHILDREN

Study this Book of Instruction continually. Meditate on it day and night so you will be sure to obey everything written in it. Only then will you prosper and succeed in all you do.
Joshua 1:8

If you have tried praying and got stuck, or you don't know where to start, the Bible is always a great place to get prayer points.

One of the best ways to pray is to pray the Scriptures. This means literally reciting God's Word back to Him. When you pray using the Scriptures, you can be confident that you are truly praying the mind of God. What greater assurance could there be?

The rain and snow come down from the heavens and stay on the ground to water the earth. They cause the grain to grow, producing seed for the farmer and bread for the hungry. It is the same with my word. I send it out, and it always produces fruit. It will accomplish all I want it to, and it will prosper everywhere I send it. Isaiah 55: 10,11

Likewise, the Spirit also helps in our weaknesses. For we do not know what we should pray for as we ought, but the Spirit Himself makes intercession for us with groanings which cannot be uttered. Romans 8:26

Praying with the Scriptures involves reading a passage of Scripture, pausing after each verse or section, and then praying about what you have read, either verbatim or in your own words. This helps you meditate on God's Word and allows it to shape your prayers.

- **Verbatim prayers:** means using the exact words of a Bible passage as your prayer, essentially speaking God's Word back to Him, literally. Praying verbatim aligns your prayers with God's will, assuring you of praying in God's will.

  For example, you might pray Psalm 23:1, "*The Lord is my shepherd, I shall not want,*" or Romans 8:28, "*And we know that for those who love God all things work together for good*", as

SCRIPTURAL AFFIRMATIONS FOR YOUR CHILDREN

it is written.

While you can pray Scripture verbatim, it is also common to personalise or adapt the verses to your specific needs and circumstances.

- **Personalised prayers:** involve taking a Scripture passage and rephrasing it in your own words, often incorporating your specific situation or needs. One amazing thing about the Bible is how the same Scripture can mean different things to you in different seasons; so with personalised prayers, you get to explore prayer points from the Scriptures in various ways.

For instance, in personalising Psalm 23:1, you might pray, *"Lord, I'm struggling with financial anxiety today, but I know you are my shepherd and I lack nothing. Please guide me and give me peace,* just as Psalm 23 promises".

Regardless of the prayer style you choose, the point is to use the Scripture as your prayer foundation and allow the Holy Spirit to guide your prayers. Praying this way gives you an almost endless list of prayers to pray over your children as they grow. I encourage you to explore and adapt this method as a way to pray over your children and over any circumstances you may be facing.

What Happens When You Pray Scriptures over Your Children?

Praying Scriptures, whether verbatim or personalised, is more than a spiritual discipline; it is a declaration of faith, identity, and divine alignment, and the benefits abound, both for you and for your children:

SPIRITUAL FORMATION
- Shapes children's identity in God's truth from an early age
- Builds a foundation of biblical literacy and spiritual awareness
- Reinforces God's promises as personal and relevant

MENTAL AND EMOTIONAL DEVELOPMENT
- Encourages positive thought patterns through scriptural affirmations
- Builds resilience and confidence rooted in divine truth
- Supports emotional regulation

PROTECTION AND PEACE
- Invokes God's covering and protection over their lives
- Helps children experience peace and emotional stability
- Guards their hearts and minds against fear, anxiety, and confusion

FAITH AND PRAYER LIFE
- Empowers you to pray with boldness and clarity
- Builds trust in God's character and faithfulness

SCRIPTURAL AFFIRMATIONS FOR YOUR CHILDREN

- Strengthens the parent-child bond through shared spiritual practice

TRANSFORMATION AND OBEDIENCE
- Aligns your heart with God's will and purpose
- Encourages obedience and moral integrity through scriptural truth
- Fosters a lifestyle of gratitude, humility, and compassion

Practical Prayers And Scriptural Affirmations

I have carefully curated a list of Scriptures and prayers to guide you as you pray and affirm over your children. They are slightly different from the previous chapters because all the prayers and affirmations are from the Scriptures. Set specific times to read these Scriptures and pray them for each of your children. May the seeds of prayers sown yield multiple results in Jesus' name. Amen.

First, is the inspiration behind this book and its title – **Psalms 144:12**. To me, it is more than a title; it is a calling, a charge, a vision of what God wants for our children.

May our sons flourish in their youth like well-nurtured plants. May our daughters be like graceful pillars, carved to beautify a palace.

FLOURISHING AND GRACEFUL

Bible Passage	Prayers/Affirmations
Psalms 144:12 NLT *May our sons flourish in their youth like well-nurtured plants. May our daughters be like graceful pillars, carved to beautify a palace.*	In Jesus' name, my children flourish as plants in their youth, they are fresh and evergreen; and like pillars sculptured in palace style, they stand regal, graceful, solid, and unmovable
Isaiah 54:13 NLT *I will teach all your children, and they will enjoy great peace.*	Father, grant [child's name] a heart that leans into Your teaching. May they delight in Your Word, walk in Your ways, and know a deep, lasting peace that guards their heart and mind.
Hosea 14:9 *For the ways of the Lord are right; The righteous walk in them, But transgressors stumble in them.*	In Jesus' name, my children walk in Your perfect ways; they are steady, secure, and upheld by Your righteousness.
Psalm 51:10 *Create in me a clean heart, O God, And renew a steadfast spirit within me.*	In Jesus' name, my child has a pure heart and a steadfast spirit; he is not deterred by worldliness. His mind is renewed daily by Your grace and truth.
John 3:16 *For God so loved the world that He gave His only begotten Son,*	In Jesus' name, my children will always believe in God. They accept

SCRIPTURAL AFFIRMATIONS FOR YOUR CHILDREN

that whoever believes in Him should not perish but have everlasting life.

the gift of God to mankind, Jesus, so they will never perish but have everlasting life, secure in Your love.

Psalm 55:22
Cast your burden on the Lord, And He shall sustain you.

In Jesus' name, my children cast their fear and weight on You. They do not experience mental disorders. You sustain and uphold them with Your strong right hand.

Isaiah 46:3-4
Listen to Me, O house of Jacob, And all the remnant of the house of Israel, Who have been upheld by Me from birth... Even to your old age, I am He, And even to gray hairs I will carry you!..

Father, you uphold my children from the moment of their conception. Carry them through every season - infancy, youth, and beyond. Your arms are their everlasting refuge; You will never let them fall.

2 Thessalonians 3:3
But the Lord is faithful, who will establish you and guard you from the evil one.

Lord Jesus, establish [children name] in Your faithfulness. Guard their steps; protect their thoughts. Surround them with Your hedge of protection so no scheme of the enemy can harm them.

2 Thessalonians 3:5
Now may the Lord direct your hearts into the love of God and into the patience of Christ.

Father, direct my child's heart into the depth of Your love and fill them with Christ-like patience. When challenges come, may he respond in grace and perseverance.

FLOURISHING AND GRACEFUL

Colossians 1:9–10
...we do not cease to pray for you, that you may be filled with the knowledge of His will in all wisdom and spiritual understanding; that you may walk worthy of the Lord... being fruitful in every good work and increasing in the knowledge of God.

Dear God, give [child's name] a complete knowledge of Your will in all wisdom and spiritual understanding. May [he/she] live worthy of Christ, producing good fruit, and growing ever deeper in the knowledge of You.

Mark 12:30–31
And you shall love the LORD your God with all your heart, with all your soul, with all your mind, and with all your strength.' This is the first commandment. And the second, like it, is this: 'You shall love your neighbor as yourself...'

Lord, ignite [child's name]'s love for You above all things. Teach [him/her] to love others with the same compassion and grace You have shown us, reflecting Your heart in every relationship.

Ephesians 4:29
Let no corrupt word proceed out of your mouth, but what is good for necessary edification, that it may impart grace to the hearers.

[Child's name], your tongue speaks life; from your lips are words of encouragement, truth, and grace. You speak with wisdom and your speech builds up others and brings glory to God's name.

Joshua 1:9
Be strong and of good courage; do not be afraid... for the Lord

Almighty God, fill [child's name] with strength and courage. When fear knocks, remind [him/her] that You go before them. May Your

SCRIPTURAL AFFIRMATIONS FOR YOUR CHILDREN

your God is with you wherever you go.

presence be their confidence and shield all the days of their life.

Matthew 28:18–20
And Jesus came and spoke to them, saying, 'All authority has been given to Me in heaven and on earth. Go therefore and make disciples of all the nations, baptizing them in the name of the Father and of the Son and of the Holy Spirit…

Lord Jesus, empower [children name] to know Your authority in heaven and earth. Send them out with bold faith to share Your love and truth, assured that You are with them always.

Philippians 4:6–7 NIV
Do not be anxious about anything, but in every situation, by prayer and petition, with thanksgiving, present your requests to God. And the peace of God, which transcends all understanding, will guard your hearts and your minds in Christ Jesus.

Father, teach [child's name] to bring every worry, question, and hope to You in prayer. Fill them with Your transcendent peace that guards their heart and mind in Christ Jesus.

Proverbs 3:5-6
Trust in the Lord with all your heart, And lean not on your own understanding; In all your ways acknowledge Him, And He shall direct your paths.

Father, I declare that [child's name] trusts You with all their heart. They do not rely on their own understanding but seek Your wisdom in every decision. You guide their steps and lead them in paths of righteousness.

FLOURISHING AND GRACEFUL

Psalm 119:11
Your word I have hidden in my heart, That I might not sin against You.

[Child's name], your heart is a treasure chest of God's Word. You walk in purity and truth, resisting temptation and choosing righteousness.

Isaiah 40:31

But those who wait on the Lord Shall renew their strength; They shall mount up with wings like eagles…

Lord, teach [child's name] to wait on You. Renew their strength daily. May they soar above discouragement and weariness, rising with boldness and grace like eagles.

James 1:5

If any of you lacks wisdom, let him ask of God… and it will be given to him.

Father, pour out Your wisdom on [child's name]. May they seek You in every challenge and receive divine insight that surpasses human understanding.

Romans 12:2

…be transformed by the renewing of your mind…

[Child's name], your mind is renewed daily by God's truth. You are not conformed to the world but transformed to reflect Christ's heart and purpose. Amen.

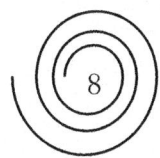

GENERATIONAL PRAYER LEGACIES

Therefore, know that the LORD your God, He is God, the faithful God who keeps covenant and mercy for a thousand generations with those who love Him and keep His commandments.
Deuteronomy 7:9

The Power of A Parent's Prayers Across Generations

I am a second-generation Christian. My great-grandparents worshipped idols. My grandparents knew only the gods of wood and stone.

Growing up, I heard my parents say repeatedly, "*We must pray.*"

FLOURISHING AND GRACEFUL

"We depend on God only for help, breakthrough, and everything." At the time, I did not fully grasp what they meant. But as I grew older and met people from multi-generational Christian families, people whose great-great-grandparents walked with God, I began to see the difference. I saw the fruit of sustained faithfulness. I saw the impact of prayers prayed decades before I was born.

This stirred something in my heart. I wanted that for my children.

I want my family line to know God, not just my children, but their children, and their children's children, even to the tenth generation, if Jesus tarries. I want to be the generation that laid the foundation, the one who broke what needed breaking and built what needed building.

Here is what I have learned: **Every multi-generational Christian family started with one generation that decided to pray differently.** Someone had to be the first. For my family, that was my parents. And now, it is my turn to carry the torch and pass it forward.

This chapter is about understanding the weight and wonder of what we are building when we pray for our children. It is about recognising that our prayers don't just affect today, they echo into eternity. It is about becoming the generation that turns the tide, lays the foundation, and sets the trajectory for those who will come after us.

Some of you will rebuild the ancient ruins; you will restore the

GENERATIONAL PRAYER LEGACIES

foundations laid long ago; you will be called the repairer of broken walls, the restorer of streets where people live. Isaiah 58:12 CSB

So, whether you are a first-generation believer like me, or you are carrying forward a legacy that is already generations deep, this is your invitation: **Pray with the future in mind. Pray for generations you will never meet. Pray like your great-great-grandchildren's faith depends on it, because it just might.**

The Bible reveals an important truth: a parent's prayers and faithfulness do not stop with their children, they create spiritual momentum that reverberates through generations.

Abraham's covenant with God established a nation. David's prayers still shapes worship today. Lois and Eunice's faith in Timothy continues to inspire the church today. These parents did not just raise good kids; their intentional spiritual parenting became the foundation upon which God built nations, kingdoms, and ultimately, His redemptive plan for humanity.

In this chapter, we will explore the parenting journeys of key biblical figures who left legacies of generational faith. You will learn practical lessons from their lives, see patterns emerge, and hopefully(this is my utmost desire) believe that **if they could do it, so can you.**

Abraham: The Father of Faith and Generational Covenant

Abraham's relationship with God

Abraham's story begins with a divine call and a promise. God said to him, "*Go from your country, your people and your father's household to the land I will show you. I will make you into a great nation, and I will bless you; I will make your name great, and you will be a blessing*" (Genesis 12:1-2 NIV).

What set Abraham apart was not perfection. Scripture records his failures honestly, but also his deep, trusting relationship with God. He is called "God's friend" (James 2:23) and the "father of all who believe" (Romans 4:11). This intimacy with God became the spiritual inheritance he would pass to his descendants.

Abraham's intercession for his children

Abraham's prayers for his children reveal a father's heart aligned with God's purposes. His most powerful act of prayer-filled parenting came through his obedience and trust. When God tested him by asking him to sacrifice Isaac, Abraham's faith demonstrated his belief that God would honour His covenant promises (Genesis 22). This was a father teaching his son practically that God is faithful, even when circumstances seem impossible.

The covenant: a prayer answered across Millennia

God established His covenant with Abraham, declaring: "I will establish my covenant as an everlasting covenant between me and you and your descendants after you for the generations to come, to be your God and the God of your descendants after you" (Genesis 17:7 NIV).

This covenant was not just for Abraham; it was explicitly intergenerational, and the impact includes:
- Isaac received the covenant blessing (Genesis 26:3-4)
- Jacob (Israel) carried it forward (Genesis 28:13-15)
- The twelve tribes emerged, becoming God's chosen nation
- Ultimately, through Abraham's lineage came Jesus Christ, through whom "all peoples on earth will be blessed" (Genesis 12:3)

Lessons from Abraham's example

1. **Your relationship with God is your greatest legacy**: Abraham's faith became the model for his descendants. Hebrews 11:8-12 celebrates his faith, and his example inspired generations to trust God.

2. **Obedience demonstrates faith to your children**: Abraham's willingness to obey God, even in the test with Isaac, taught his son that God could be trusted completely.

3. **Covenant promises extend beyond your lifetime**: Abraham died seeing only a fraction of God's promises fulfilled, yet his prayers and faith set a trajectory that continues today.

David: A Man after God's Heart

David's prayer for Solomon

One of the most powerful prayers in Scripture for a child comes from David as he prepared to pass his throne to Solomon. This prayer set the tone for Solomon's rule as king.

And give my son Solomon the wholehearted devotion to keep your commands, your statutes and your decrees and to do everything to build the palatial structure for which I have provided. 1 Chronicles 29:19 NIV

Key elements of David's prayer

- Wholehearted devotion: David prayed for Solomon's heart condition, not just his behaviour. He understood that external obedience flows from internal devotion.
- Obedience to God's Word: He specifically prayed that Solomon would keep God's commands, statutes, and decrees, recognising that knowing and following Scripture was essential.
- Completion of divine calling: David prayed for Solomon to fulfil the specific purpose God had for him, building the temple that David was not permitted to build.

The Davidic covenant: a prayer legacy

God made a covenant with David that paralleled Abraham's in its generational scope:

When your days are over and you rest with your ancestors, I will raise up your offspring to succeed you, your own flesh and blood, and I will

GENERATIONAL PRAYER LEGACIES

establish his kingdom. He is the one who will build a house for my Name, and I will establish the throne of his kingdom forever. I will be his father, and he will be my son. 2 Samuel 7:12-14a NIV

This covenant promise had immediate fulfilment in Solomon but ultimate fulfilment in Jesus Christ, the eternal King from David's line.

Lessons from David's example

1. **Pray for your children's hearts, not just their behaviour**: David asked for "wholehearted devotion" for Solomon, understanding that heart transformation is the foundation of godly living.
2. **Verbalise your faith and expectations**: David did not assume Solomon would know God's ways; he explicitly instructed him and connected obedience to blessing.
3. **Prepare your children for their unique calling**: David prayed specifically for Solomon to accomplish what God had called him to do - build the temple.
4. **Connect present obedience to future generations**: David helped Solomon see that his faithfulness would impact his children and grandchildren.
5. **Model repentance and restoration**: Though David sinned grievously, he also showed his sons what it meant to repent genuinely and be restored to God.
6. **Prayer does not override free will**: Each generation must choose to follow God; even Solomon, who began so well, got carried away by his idolatrous wives.
7. **Parental prayers and legacy still bear fruit**: Despite Solomon's failures, God's covenant with David remained, and the promise ultimately led to Christ.

Lois And Eunice: A Mother & Grandmother's Legacy of Sincere Faith

The power of a woman's spiritual influence

While Abraham and David demonstrate powerful examples of fathers praying for and spiritually investing in their children, the story of Lois, Eunice, and Timothy reveals the profound impact of mothers and grandmothers who faithfully pass on their faith across generations, even in challenging circumstances.

Their story: faith in difficult ground

Eunice was a Jewish believer married to a Greek man who apparently did not share her faith (Acts 16:1). Her cultural context presented significant challenges to raising a child in the Jewish faith and later in Christian belief. Despite this obstacle, Eunice, alongside her mother Lois, created a home environment where genuine faith could flourish. We may not know the details of their daily lives, but we know the result - Timothy, who became one of Paul's most trusted companions and a leader in the early church.

Eunice's situation represents a reality many mothers face: a spiritually divided home. Her circumstances presented enormous challenges you may also relate to:

- Cultural pressure: Greek culture dominated their city of Lystra, a pressure that parents raising children in the diaspora may be familiar with
- Limited authority: In patriarchal societies where fathers typically determined their children's religious training, it took courage to disciple her son in the faith
- Isolation: She may have felt alone in her desire to raise Timothy in faith
- Doubt: She might have wondered if her influence would be enough

Yet the outcome proves that a faithful mother (and grandmother) can successfully pass on faith even when the father is not spiritually leading the home. This offers profound hope to single mothers, widows, and women married to unbelievers.

The generational flow: from grandmother to mother to son

I am reminded of your sincere faith, which first lived in your grandmother Lois and in your mother Eunice and, I am persuaded, now lives in you also. 2 Timothy 1:5 NIV

Paul's words reveal a clear lineage of faith:
- Lois (Grandmother) - The faith "first lived" in her
- Eunice (Mother) - It dwelt in her as well
- Timothy (Son) - Now it lives in him

This was not genetic inheritance; faith cannot be passed

down through DNA. Rather, it demonstrates intentional spiritual investment across generations. Lois discipled Eunice, and together they discipled Timothy.

How they passed on their faith

While Scripture does not give us specific prayers Lois and Eunice prayed, we can discern their methods from the results:

1. **They Taught Scripture from Childhood**
   Paul reminds Timothy: "*From infancy you have known the Holy Scriptures, which are able to make you wise for salvation through faith in Christ Jesus*" (2 Timothy 3:15).
   "From infancy" indicates that Eunice and Lois began Timothy's spiritual education from his earliest days. Despite living in a predominantly Greek culture with an unbelieving father, they prioritised teaching him the Torah, the Jewish Scriptures.

2. **They Modelled Authentic Faith**
   Paul does not just mention that they taught Timothy about faith; he notes that faith "lived" in them first.
   Children learn more from what they see than what they are told. Timothy could have followed his father's example and observed pagan rites, but he accepted the Jewish faith and teaching of his godly mother and grandmother. Their genuine, daily walk with God was the curriculum Timothy absorbed most powerfully.

3. **They Prayed for and over Him**
   Though not explicitly stated, Jewish mothers and grandmothers of this era would have prayed daily for

their children. Given the result, Timothy's "sincere faith", we can be confident that Lois and Eunice bathed Timothy in prayer throughout his childhood and beyond.

4. **They Prepared Him for His Calling**
   When Paul met Timothy and invited him to join his missionary team (Acts 16:1-3), Timothy was ready. He had been prepared spiritually, intellectually, and practically. This preparation was not accidental; it was the fruit of years of intentional spiritual parenting.

The outcome: a spiritual leader emerges
Timothy went on to:
- Become Paul's trusted companion and fellow worker (Philippians 2:19-22)
- Lead the church in Ephesus, one of the most important early Christian communities
- Receive two canonical letters from Paul (1 and 2 Timothy) that have guided church leaders for 2,000 years
- Be remembered as a model of faithful ministry and genuine devotion to Christ

Paul wrote of Timothy: "*I have no one else like him, who will show genuine concern for your welfare*" (Philippians 2:20, NIV). This "genuine concern" echoed the "sincere faith" he learned from his mother and grandmother.

Lessons from Lois and Eunice's example

1. **Your Faith Must Be Authentic**: Their faith was genuine, real and not just something polished. Children have an uncanny ability to detect hypocrisy. What you live matters more than what you say.

2. **Start Early and Be Consistent**: Timothy knew the Scriptures "from infancy." Don't wait until your children are older to begin their spiritual formation. The early years are foundational.

3. **Grandmothers Matter Too**: Lois is mentioned first in Paul's account, suggesting her significant influence. Grandparents who invest spiritually in their grandchildren create a powerful double witness of faith. If you are a grandmother, your prayers and involvement are essential.

4. **You Can Succeed Even in Difficult Circumstances**: Eunice did not have an ideal situation, yet she succeeded in passing on her faith. Your circumstances do not disqualify you; God's grace is sufficient.

5. **Teach Scripture Intentionally**: Lois and Eunice did not leave Timothy's biblical education to chance or to the synagogue alone. Regular, consistent exposure to Scripture in the home is irreplaceable.

6. **Your Investment Will Multiply**: When Timothy left home to travel with Paul and minister in churches, he left with his own faith, not his mother's or grandmother's. The goal is not to create dependency but to launch your children into their own authentic relationship with God. And when that happens, they can impact thousands, as Timothy did.

GENERATIONAL PRAYER LEGACIES

Common Themes in Their Spiritual Parenting

1. **Covenant Relationship with God**
   Abraham and David operated from a foundation of covenant relationship with God. Their prayers were not manipulative attempts to get God to do what they wanted, they were collaborative conversations with a God who had already committed Himself to them and their descendants. Lois and Eunice, though not recipients of direct covenant promises like Abraham and David, operated from the same covenantal framework, the promises made to Israel that they believed and lived out daily.

2. **Intentionality**
   None of these parents left their children's spiritual formation to chance. Abraham, David, Lois, and Eunice all spoke about God, prayed for their children, and created environments where encountering God was normal. Timothy knew Scripture "from infancy" because Eunice and Lois were intentional. Solomon knew what God required because David was intentional.

3. **Imperfect Parents, Perfect God**
   Abraham and David failed as fathers in various ways. Abraham sent Hagar and Ishmael away. David's family life was marked by dysfunction, neglect of some

children, failure to discipline, and multiple wives, causing rivalry. Lois and Eunice's failures were not documented. Yet God's faithfulness to their children shone through, despite their imperfections.

4. **Authentic Faith, Not Performance**
Paul describes Lois and Eunice's faith as sincere without hypocrisy. This echoes what made Abraham and David stand out: a genuine relationship with God, not religious performance. Abraham was called God's friend. David was a man after God's own heart. All four modelled authentic faith that their children could recognise as real.

5. **Long-Term Vision**
Abraham, David, Lois, and Eunice all had a multi-generational perspective. They understood that their faithfulness was planting seeds for a harvest their grandchildren and great-grandchildren would reap. Timothy went on to mentor others, continuing the generational chain. And we are still singing "Abraham's blessings are mine" today.

6. **Scripture as Foundation**
Where specifically mentioned, all these parents grounded their children in God's Word. David charged Solomon to keep God's commands, statutes, and decrees. Lois and Eunice taught Timothy the Scriptures from infancy. The Word of God was central to their spiritual parenting.

GENERATIONAL PRAYER LEGACIES

The Generational Ripple Effect

From Abraham's prayers:
- Isaac learned to trust God and received the covenant blessing
- Jacob encountered God personally and was transformed
- Joseph's faith in Egypt saved nations and preserved God's people
- Centuries later, Jesus, the ultimate fulfilment of blessing to all nations, came through Abraham's line

From Lois and Eunice's prayers:
- Timothy developed sincere faith from infancy
- He became Paul's most trusted companion in ministry
- He led the church at Ephesus, influencing countless believers
- His legacy continues through Paul's letters to him, teaching pastors and leaders for over 2,000 years

One generation's faithful prayers and spiritual investment become the next generation's foundation, which becomes the following generation's springboard. When parents and grandparents genuinely walk with God and intentionally pass on their faith, they set a trajectory that can impact the world.

God's covenant with Abraham resulted in Jesus Christ, the Saviour of the world, appearing some 2,000 years after Abraham's death. David's prayers for Solomon and his descendants ultimately pointed to Jesus, the eternal King on David's throne. Lois and Eunice's faithful teaching of Timothy produced a church leader whose legacy continues through

Scripture itself.

Whether you are a father like Abraham or David, a mother like Eunice, or a grandmother like Lois, whether you are in an ideal situation or facing difficult circumstances, your sincere faith and faithful prayers can shape not only your children but their children and their children's children.

Your children's names are known to God. Your prayers for them rise before His throne. Your faithfulness plants seeds that may bloom in your grandchildren, great-grandchildren, and beyond. In God's economy, no prayer for your children is wasted, no act of faithful parenting is insignificant.

As you pray for your children, you join a company of faithful parents stretching back through Timothy's grandmother Lois and mother Eunice, through David, through Abraham, through all the generations who have entrusted their children to the God of the covenant, the God who keeps His promises to a thousand generations of those who love Him.

A Prayer for Praying Parents:

Lord, as Abraham, David, Lois, and Eunice entrusted their children to You, I bring my children before You now. Give me wholehearted devotion to You so that I may model genuine, sincere faith.

Give my children hearts that seek You, wisdom that follows Your ways, and courage to walk in their calling. Let Your Word dwell richly in them from their earliest days.

Establish Your covenant promises in their lives and in their children's lives for generations to come. Where I fail, be faithful. Where I am weak, be strong. Where my circumstances are difficult, be sufficient.

Let the prayers I pray today bear fruit in my great-grandchildren's lives. I trust You with my most precious treasures. In Jesus' name, Amen.

"

Good parenting is contagious. Your children will become parents much like you. What you're doing or not doing will trickle down from generation to generation.

—

Dr. Lawson Murray

Appendix A: Emergency Prayers for Crisis Situations

How to Use These Prayers

Crisis moments require immediate, powerful intercession. These prayers are designed for urgent situations when you need to cry out to God quickly and effectively.

The LORD is near to all who call on him, to all who call on him in truth. Psalm 145:18

In moments of crisis:
- Pray these prayers out loud with authority
- Declare Scripture over the situation
- Don't wait for perfect words, God hears your heart
- Call on other believers to pray in agreement with you
- Trust that God is already at work even before you pray

MEDICAL EMERGENCIES & HEALTH CRISES

When Your Child Is Sick or Injured

Immediate Prayer:
"Dear God, I come to You in Jesus' name. You are Jehovah Rapha, the God who heals. I speak healing over [child's name]'s body right now. You knit them together in the womb, and You know every cell, every organ, every system. I command this

FLOURISHING AND GRACEFUL

sickness/injury to leave in Jesus' name. Send Your healing power. Guide the doctors' hands and give them supernatural wisdom. Protect [child's name] from complications, infections, and further harm. I declare Psalm 103:3 over them: You forgive all their sins and heal all their diseases. Thank You that by Jesus' stripes, [child's name] is healed. I receive Your healing now, in Jesus' mighty name. Amen."

Scripture to Declare:
- "He himself bore our sins in his body on the cross, so that we might die to sins and live for righteousness; by his wounds you have been healed." — 1 Peter 2:24
- "I will restore you to health and heal your wounds, declares the LORD." — Jeremiah 30:17
- "The prayer offered in faith will make the sick person well; the Lord will raise them up." — James 5:15

When Facing a Frightening Diagnosis

Immediate Prayer:
"Lord, I refuse to fear. You have not given me a spirit of fear, but of power, love, and a sound mind (2 Timothy 1:7). This diagnosis is not the final word—You are. I place [child's name] in Your hands. You are the God who does the impossible. I stand on Your promises: You will restore their health and let them live. I speak life over [child's name]. I cancel every negative report that contradicts Your Word. Give us wisdom for treatment decisions, supernatural peace in the waiting, and faith that doesn't waver. We will see Your goodness in the land of the living. In Jesus' name, Amen."

Appendix A

Scripture to Declare:
- "But I will restore you to health and heal your wounds, declares the LORD." —Jeremiah 30:17
- "Do not be anxious about anything, but in every situation, by prayer and petition, with thanksgiving, present your requests to God." — Philippians 4:6
- "The LORD sustains them on their sickbed and restores them from their bed of illness." — Psalm 41:3

When A Loved One Has Been in An Accident

Immediate Prayer:
Dear God, I cry out to You over [person's name]! Be with them right now. Protect their life. Sustain their body. Send skilled medical personnel. Prevent internal injuries, bleeding, brain damage, and trauma. Calm their fear. Give them Your peace that surpasses understanding. I speak stabilisation over their vitals. Cover them with Your protection. Perform miracles, Lord. Do what only You can do. I trust You with [person's name]'s life. Thank You that You are already at work. In Jesus' name, Amen."

Scripture to Declare:
- "Even though I walk through the darkest valley, I will fear no evil, for you are with me." — Psalm 23:4
- "God is our refuge and strength, an ever-present help in trouble." — Psalm 46:1
- "He will cover you with his feathers, and under his wings you will find refuge." — Psalm 91:4

FLOURISHING AND GRACEFUL

SPIRITUAL WARFARE & ATTACK

When Your Child Is Under Spiritual Attack

Immediate Prayer:
"Father, I stand in the gap for [child's name]. The enemy has launched an attack, but greater is He who is in us than he who is in the world. I plead the blood of Jesus over [child's name]. I bind every demonic force, every spirit of confusion, rebellion, darkness, and destruction assigned against them. I cancel every assignment of the enemy in Jesus' name. I declare that [child's name] belongs to God. No weapon formed against them will prosper. I cover their mind, their heart, their spirit, and their physical body with the full armour of God. Holy Spirit, surround them with Your presence. Dispatch warring angels on their behalf. Break every chain. Shatter every stronghold. Set them free. In the mighty name of Jesus, Amen."

Scripture to Declare:
- "No weapon forged against you will prevail." — Isaiah 54:17
- "The one who is in you is greater than the one who is in the world." — 1 John 4:4
- "Submit yourselves, then, to God. Resist the devil, and he will flee from you." — James 4:7

Also, pray the prayer of the full armour (Ephesians 6:10-18). **Ref:** Chapter 5 of this book

Appendix A

When Your Child Is Being Influenced by Darkness

Immediate Prayer:
"Lord, I see the enemy's influence in [child's name]'s life, and I stand against it. I break every ungodly soul tie, every demonic influence, every open door that has given the enemy access. I cancel every agreement [child's name] has made with darkness—knowingly or unknowingly. Holy Spirit, convict them. Open their eyes to see the truth. Give them the desire to turn away from darkness and turn toward Your light. Surround them with godly influences. Remove toxic relationships. Expose every hidden thing. Deliver them from evil. I claim [child's name] for the Kingdom of God. They will serve You all the days of their life. In Jesus' name, Amen."

Scripture to Declare:
- "If we confess our sins, he is faithful and just and will forgive us our sins and purify us from all unrighteousness." — 1 John 1:9
- "For he has rescued us from the dominion of darkness and brought us into the kingdom of the Son he loves." — Colossians 1:13
- "Therefore, if anyone is in Christ, the new creation has come: The old has gone, the new is here!" — 2 Corinthians 5:17

FLOURISHING AND GRACEFUL

GRIEF & LOSS

When You Are Grieving

Immediate Prayer:
"Father, my heart is broken, and so is [person's name]. You are near to the brokenhearted. Comfort us in this loss. Wrap us in Your loving arms. Help us process this pain in healthy ways. Surround us with Your comfort and support. Give us the right words—or the wisdom to just be present in silence. Heal our hearts over time. Help us remember that this is not the end of the story. You will redeem even this. You will work all things together for good. Hold us close, Lord. In Jesus' name, Amen."

Scripture to Declare:
- "The LORD is close to the brokenhearted and saves those who are crushed in spirit." — Psalm 34:18
- "Blessed are those who mourn, for they will be comforted." — Matthew 5:4
- "He heals the brokenhearted and binds up their wounds." — Psalm 147:3

PRAYERS FOR PARENTS IN CRISIS

When You Feel Like You're Failing as a Parent

Prayer for Yourself:
"Father, I'm struggling. I feel like I'm failing [child's name]. I don't have the answers. I'm exhausted, overwhelmed, and discouraged. But I'm bringing my inadequacy to You. You

Appendix A

chose me to be [child's name]'s parent. Give me Your strength, Your wisdom, Your grace. Help me to parent out of Your abundance, not my lack. Remind me that You don't expect perfection—You expect dependence. Forgive my mistakes. Redeem my failures. Give me hope for tomorrow. I can't do this alone, but I can do it with You. In Jesus' name, Amen."*

Scripture to Declare:
"My grace is sufficient for you, for my power is made perfect in weakness." — 2 Corinthians 12:9
"I can do all this through him who gives me strength." — Philippians 4:13
"Cast all your anxiety on him because he cares for you." — 1 Peter 5:7

A WORD OF ENCOURAGEMENT

Crisis prayers are not prayers of last resort; they are prayers of **first response**. When you do not know what to do, God does. When you cannot fix it, God can. When you are at the end of yourself, you are at the beginning of His miraculous help. Remember:

- God hears you the moment you call
- No crisis is too big for Him
- He loves your child even more than you do
- He is already at work before you pray
- Your prayers are powerful and effective

"Call to me and I will answer you and tell you great and unsearchable things you do not know." — Jeremiah 33:3

Appendix B: Leading Your Child to Christ

One of the greatest joys of parenting is seeing your child come to know Jesus personally. Beyond providing love, education, and opportunities, the most eternal investment you can make is to lead your child into a living relationship with God.

This appendix will guide you in how to explain salvation in simple terms, pray with your child, and nurture their growing faith.

1. **Preparing Their Hearts**
   Children come to faith at different ages and levels of understanding. Your role is not to pressure them but to create an environment where Jesus feels real and approachable.

   You prepare their hearts by:
   • Modelling your own faith daily (through prayer, kindness, and forgiveness).
   • Talking about Jesus naturally during everyday moments like meals, bedtime, and car rides.
   • Reading the Bible together and highlighting God's love and purpose for them.
   • Praying with and for them, allowing them to see faith as relational, not religious.

Appendix B

2. **Explaining the Gospel Simply**
   You do not need theological depth to explain salvation to them; just truth, clarity, and love. Here is how to share the message of salvation in simple terms:

   - God loves you. "God made you, loves you, and wants to be your forever friend." (John 3:16)
   - Sin separates us from God. *"Sometimes we do wrong things — that's called sin — and it keeps us from God."* (Romans 3:23)
   - Jesus took our place. *"Jesus came to earth, died on the cross for our sins, and rose again so we can be close to God."* (Romans 5:8)
   - We can choose to follow Him. *"If you believe in Jesus and invite Him into your heart, He will forgive you and live in you forever."* (Romans 10:9,10)

   Keep the conversation open, using their language and examples they understand (e.g., forgiveness, love, friendship).

3. **Leading Them in a Simple Prayer**
   If your child expresses readiness and understanding, you can guide them through a prayer like this:

   "Dear Jesus, thank You for loving me. I know I have done wrong things and need Your forgiveness.
   Thank You for dying for my sins and rising again.

Today, I ask You to come into my heart and be my Lord and Saviour.
Help me to live for You and love You all my life.
Thank You for making me Your child. Amen."

Rejoice with them afterwards, this is a special moment! Encourage them that salvation is the beginning of a lifelong friendship with Jesus.

4. **Nurturing Their Faith**

Now begins the beautiful journey of discipleship. Help your child grow by:
- Reading the Bible together (start with John, Psalms, Proverbs, or stories about Jesus).
- Praying daily as a family.
- Attending church and children's fellowship regularly.
- Talking about what they learn from Scripture.
- Celebrating spiritual milestones like baptism, answered prayers, or faith decisions.

A Parent's Prayer:

"Lord Jesus, thank You for the gift of my child. Thank You for drawing them to Yourself. Help me to nurture their faith with wisdom, patience, and grace. Give me words that plant seeds of truth, and a life that reflects Your love. May my child walk with You all their days and bring glory to Your name. Amen."

A WORD OF ENCOURAGEMENT

Do not worry or be anxious if your child does not respond immediately or seems unsure. Continue praying, modelling faith, and trusting the Holy Spirit's timing.

Acknowledgement

Writing a book about intentional parenting and prayer while learning the ropes myself has been one of the most humbling and empowering experiences of my life.

First, all glory to God, who placed this burden on my heart and gave me the grace to see it through. Every word on these pages is a testimony of Your faithfulness.

To Samson, my 'bestest' partner, my greatest cheerleader, and my sounding board—thank you for toiling alongside me in prayer, in parenting, and in this project. Your faithfulness, sacrifice, and intentionality inspire me daily. I could not have done this without you.

To our son, AmiifeOluwa—you are the reason this book exists. Watching you grow has been my greatest joy. This book is for you and every child out there. Every prayer in this book was written with your face in mind.

To my parents—your prayers laid the foundation for my faith. Thank you for never stopping to pray for me. The seeds you sowed have grown into mighty trees, and now others are blessed by the shade.

To my pastor, Pastor Kenny—thank you for believing in me, encouraging me, and writing the foreword to this book. Your wisdom and guidance are woven throughout these pages.

To Sis Angela—I am so grateful for your words of wisdom, your ginger, and your 'cane' (you know what I mean!). Thank you for always rooting for me and pushing me to aim higher. I call you blessed.

To Chioma and my Ladilak Girls—thank you for your encouragement, reviews, accountability, and prayers that carried me through every task and deadline. You held my arms up when they grew weary.

To my community members, both at home and abroad, and to everyone whose stories inspired me—your vulnerability gave this book its heartbeat. Thank you for trusting me with your struggles and victories, and for holding me up in your prayers. Your stories will bless countless families.

And to you, holding this book right now—God knew you would be reading these words today. He has already gone before you, preparing the way for a breakthrough in your family. I pray that you will discover the joy, power, and privilege of being a praying parent.

May the Lord bless you and your household as you commit to praying intentionally and effectively for your children.

Personal Notes & Prayers

Personal Notes & Prayers

Personal Notes & Prayers

Personal Notes & Prayers

About The Author

Esther Ojosemako is a writer, speaker, and Abba's daughter passionate about helping believers, live with purpose and intentionality. A software professional turned author, Esther combines her analytical mind and deep spiritual insight to create resources that nurture growth, wellness, and faith in everyday life.

She is the author of **Love Letters to Abba** and **The Prayer Journal**, both of which inspires readers to deepen their relationship with God through gratitude and prayer. **Flourishing & Graceful: A Praying Guide for Intentional Parents** was born out of Esther's journey into motherhood and her desire to raise children anchored in faith and divine purpose.

Through her platform, **The Esthitude Place**, she continues to share reflections, insights, and practical wisdom that equip her followers to thrive spiritually and emotionally. Esther lives with her husband and son, finding daily joy in faith, family, and the grace to flourish.

Get The Praying Parent Tooklit

If you enjoyed reading this book, you will appreciate this toolkit designed to accompany you in your intentional parenting journey.

Scan the QR code below to access it.

Scan The QR Code below to Access Other Books & Resources by The Author

Scan me!

Contact the author:
esthitudeplace.com
@esthitude_ | @theesthitudeplace

Printed in Dunstable, United Kingdom